Viral Blueprints for Small Busin

Social Media Marketing

By

Dr. David K. Ewen

Enterprise College

Copyright © 2025, Dr. David K. Ewen of Enterprise College. All rights reserved.

This content may not be copied, reproduced, distributed, transmitted, displayed, published, or broadcast without the prior written permission of the copyright holder. Published by Enterprise College founded by Dr. David K. Ewen

ISBN: 9798280856394

Imprint: Independently published by Enterprise College

Viral Blueprints for Small Business Success

Social Media Marketing

Dr. David K. Ewen

Table of Contents

About the Book

Viral Blueprints for Small Business Success reveals the technical strategies behind social media marketing that actually work for small businesses. The journey begins by uncovering core secrets that set successful campaigns apart from the noise. Readers learn how to build a compelling brand presence from the ground up, even with limited resources. The book dives into creating content that not only attracts attention but also forges real connections with audiences. It demystifies each major platform, showing how to tailor efforts for maximum reach and engagement. Proven growth strategies are laid out step by step, empowering readers to expand their audiences efficiently. The importance of sparking genuine conversations and building community is highlighted as a key to lasting influence. Readers discover how to harness analytics and data to refine their approach and achieve measurable results. By the final chapter, small business owners are equipped to adapt, thrive, and sustain their momentum in the ever evolving world of social media.

About the Author

Dr. David K. Ewen is a distinguished educator, entrepreneur, and ordained minister whose multifaceted career spans over three decades. Since launching his entrepreneurial journey in 1994, he has earned numerous accolades for his contributions to education, business, and community service.

As the Chancellor and President of Enterprise College, an international university specializing in global communication studies, Dr. Ewen has been instrumental in shaping curricula that address the evolving needs of global learners. His leadership emphasizes the importance of cross-cultural communication and digital literacy in today's interconnected world.

In addition to his academic endeavors, Dr. Ewen serves as the Chair of SCORE Western Massachusetts, where he leads a team of certified mentors dedicated to supporting small businesses and non-profit organizations. Through workshops and personalized mentoring, he assists entrepreneurs in areas such as planning, marketing, tax compliance, and team building.

Dr. Ewen's media presence includes a 20-year tenure as an international talk show host on platforms like Blog Talk Radio and Spotify, where he discussed topics ranging from entrepreneurship to personal development. He is also a prolific author and audiobook producer, with works covering subjects such as education, leadership, spirituality, and global affairs.

Beyond his professional achievements, Dr. Ewen is deeply committed to outreach ministry. As an ordained minister, he dedicates his time to supporting the homeless and incarcerated, providing spiritual guidance and advocating for their well-being. His compassionate approach underscores his belief in the transformative power of faith and community support.

Dr. Ewen's enduring dedication to education, entrepreneurship, and humanitarian efforts continues to inspire individuals and communities worldwide.

Chapter 1: Unlocking Social Media Marketing Secrets

Social media marketing can feel like unlocking a treasure chest without knowing where the key is hidden. Many businesses dive in, posting random content, hoping for success, but they quickly find themselves lost. The key to unlocking that treasure lies in understanding what works and why it works. Social media is not just about posting pictures or videos; it is about creating a connection. Think of it as planting a seed that needs the right care, water, and sunlight to grow into something meaningful.

Building a brand is like painting a picture on a blank canvas. You cannot just throw colors randomly and hope for a masterpiece. Instead, you need a vision, a plan, and the right tools to make it come alive. Your logo, tone of voice, and overall message are the brushes and paints you use. When everything works together, the picture becomes clear, and your audience can see and feel who you are.

Creating content for social media is like cooking a dish for a large group of people. You cannot just throw ingredients together and expect everyone to love the meal. You need to consider what your audience likes, what they need, and how you can serve something unique. For example, if your audience enjoys humor, your content should sprinkle in some jokes. If they value information, make sure your content is educational and helpful.

Each social media platform is like a different kind of party. Instagram is a visual art gallery where people love beautiful pictures. Twitter is a fast-moving conversation where short, sharp thoughts matter most. LinkedIn is a professional networking event where people share business tips and achievements. Facebook is like a big family gathering where stories are shared in detail. Knowing the type of party you are attending allows you to act and dress appropriately.

Growing an audience on social media is similar to building a garden. You cannot expect flowers to bloom overnight. You plant the seeds by creating good content, water them by engaging with your followers, and give them sunlight by staying consistent. Over time, the garden will grow, and you will see the results of your hard work. But remember, you need patience because nothing grows in a day.

Engaging with your followers is like having a conversation at a coffee shop. It is not about talking nonstop about yourself; it is about listening and responding. When someone comments on your post or sends a message, it is your chance to show them you care. For example, if a follower asks a question about your product, take the time to give them a thoughtful answer. This small act of kindness can turn a casual follower into a loyal supporter.

Sparking conversations is like lighting a campfire. At first, you need to add small sticks and gently blow on the flames to get it going. Once the fire is strong, it will provide warmth and light for everyone around it. Similarly, on social media, starting small conversations can lead to bigger, more meaningful discussions. These conversations build trust and keep your audience coming back for more.

Analyzing data on social media is like reading a map before starting a journey. Without it, you might go in circles or get lost entirely. The data tells you what is working, what is not, and where you should go next. For example, if you see that your videos perform better than your photos, you can focus more on creating videos. This insight helps guide your decisions and keeps you on the right track.

Challenges on social media are like unexpected storms during a road trip. You cannot always predict them, but you can prepare for them. Sometimes, your posts might not perform well, or you might face negative comments. These moments test your ability to adapt and stay focused on your goal. Remember, every storm passes, and the sun will shine again if you keep moving forward.

Adapting to changes is like sailing a boat on the ocean. The wind and waves are always shifting, and you need to adjust your sails to stay on course. Social media platforms often update their algorithms or introduce new features. Instead of resisting these changes, embrace them as opportunities to grow. For example, if a new platform becomes popular, learn how to use it to connect with your audience.

Sustaining growth on social media is like keeping a fire burning through the night. You need to add wood regularly and make sure the flames do not die out. Consistency is the key to staying visible and relevant to your audience. This means posting regularly, engaging with your followers, and staying true to your brand. Over time, the fire will grow stronger, and your presence will become impossible to ignore.

Social media marketing is not about instant success; it is about building something that lasts. Think of it like constructing a house brick by brick. Each post, comment, and interaction adds another brick to the foundation. If you rush or skip steps, the house might collapse. But if you take your time and do it right, you create something strong and reliable.

Your audience is like a group of friends you want to keep close. You need to nurture the relationship by showing them you care. For example, celebrate milestones with them, like reaching a follower goal or launching a new product. Share your successes and even your struggles to make them feel like part of your journey. This connection transforms followers into a loyal community.

Social media is a tool, but it is also an art. It is like playing an instrument where practice and creativity go hand in hand. The more you experiment, the better you will understand what works for your audience. For instance, testing different styles of content, such as videos, images, or polls, can reveal what engages your followers the most. Over time, you will master the rhythm that resonates with your audience.

The power of storytelling on social media is like reading a good book that you cannot put down. Stories capture attention, evoke emotions, and leave a lasting impression. Instead of just promoting your product, share the story behind it. For example, talk about how your business started or the challenges you overcame. These stories create a deeper connection with your audience.

Every post you make is like a pebble dropped into a pond. It creates ripples that spread far beyond the initial splash. A single post might reach someone who shares it with others, leading to a chain reaction. This is why it is important to craft content that is meaningful and shareable. The ripples of one good post can lead to incredible opportunities.

Timing on social media is like catching a wave while surfing. If you paddle too early or too late, you will miss the wave entirely. Posting at the right time ensures that your audience is online and ready to engage. For instance, if your audience is most active in the evening, schedule your posts during that time. Catching the right wave can make a big difference in your success.

Consistency on social media is like building muscle at the gym. You cannot go once and expect to see results. It takes regular effort, discipline, and time to see progress. Posting once a month will not keep your audience engaged, but posting consistently will. Over time, your consistent efforts will build a strong and recognizable brand.

Collaborating with others on social media is like playing in a band. Each member brings their own unique talent to the table, creating something greater together. Partnering with influencers or other businesses can expose you to new audiences. For example, a small bakery might collaborate with a local coffee shop for a joint promotion. This teamwork benefits everyone involved and amplifies the reach of your message.

Staying authentic on social media is like being yourself at a party. People can tell when you are trying too hard to impress, and it often backfires. Being genuine helps you attract the right kind of followers who truly connect with your brand. For example, sharing behind-the-scenes moments or personal stories makes you relatable and trustworthy. Authenticity is the key to building long-term relationships.

Learning from others is like standing on the shoulders of giants. Many brands have already paved the way with successful social media strategies. Observing and analyzing their methods can provide valuable insights. For instance, studying how a popular brand engages with its audience can inspire your own approach. By learning from their successes and mistakes, you can improve your own efforts.

Social media marketing requires patience, just like growing a tree. You plant the seed, water it regularly, and wait for it to grow. Success does not happen overnight, but your consistent care will eventually bear fruit. For example, a small business might start with only a few followers but grow steadily by posting quality content and engaging consistently. Patience and persistence are the keys to long-term success.

Mistakes on social media are like falling off a bicycle while learning to ride. They are inevitable, but they teach you important lessons. For example, a poorly performing post can help you understand what your audience does not like. Instead of fearing mistakes, embrace them as opportunities to grow and improve. Each mistake brings you closer to mastering social media marketing.

Chapter 2: Building Your Brand from Scratch

Building your brand from scratch is like constructing a house. You need a strong foundation to support everything else you will create. Without a solid base, the house might fall apart when challenges come. For example, your foundation is your brand's purpose and values, which guide all your decisions. When you know what your business stands for, it becomes easier to build something stable and lasting.

Choosing a name for your brand is like naming a new baby. The name has to be meaningful, memorable, and represent who you are. It should reflect what your business offers and stay in people's minds. For instance, a brand selling eco-friendly products might choose a name like "Green Roots" to show their focus on sustainability. A good name helps people connect with your brand instantly.

Your logo is like the face of your brand. It is the first thing people see, and it should leave a lasting impression. A good logo is simple, unique, and tells a story about your business. For example, a bakery might use a logo shaped like a loaf of bread to represent their products. When people see your logo, they should immediately know what your brand is about.

Building a brand identity is like choosing how to dress for an important event. The way you present yourself, such as your style and colors, says a lot about who you are. For your brand, this means creating a consistent look with fonts, colors, and designs. For example, a children's toy store might use bright colors and playful designs to show they are fun and family-friendly. A clear identity helps people recognize and remember your brand.

Your brand's voice is like the tone of a conversation. It can be friendly, serious, professional, or funny, depending on who your audience is. For example, a tech company might use a professional tone to show expertise, while a coffee shop might use a warm and casual tone to feel welcoming. Choosing the right voice helps you connect with your audience on a personal level. It makes your brand feel more human and relatable.

Defining your target audience is like picking the right audience for a play. You want to perform for the people who will enjoy and appreciate your story. For example, if you sell fitness equipment, your target audience might be people who love exercising or want to get healthier. Knowing who you are speaking to helps you create messages that resonate with them. It ensures that your efforts are not wasted on the wrong crowd.

Creating a unique selling point is like baking a signature dish that no one else can make. It is what makes your brand stand out from the competition. For example, a skincare brand might focus on using only organic ingredients, which sets them apart from others. Your unique selling point should show why customers should choose you instead of someone else. It gives your brand its own special flavor.

Your mission is like the compass that guides your journey. It points you in the right direction and keeps you focused on your goals. For example, a clothing company might have a mission to create stylish, affordable fashion while being environmentally friendly. A clear mission statement helps your team and audience understand what you are working towards. It gives your brand purpose and meaning.

Consistency in branding is like staying in character during a play. If you suddenly change your tone or message, the audience might get confused. For example, a luxury brand should always maintain an elegant and sophisticated style, even in social media posts. Consistency helps build trust and loyalty with your audience. People know what to expect from your brand, and that creates a sense of reliability.

Your online presence is like a digital storefront. It is where people go to learn more about your brand and decide if they want to engage with it. For example, a well-designed website with clear information and attractive visuals can make a great first impression. Your social media pages are also part of this storefront, showing your brand's personality and values. A strong online presence makes it easier for people to find and connect with you.

Building trust with your audience is like planting a tree and watching it grow. Trust takes time to develop, but once it is strong, it can weather any storm. For example, responding to customer questions honestly and delivering on your promises can help build trust. When people trust your brand, they are more likely to stay loyal and recommend you to others. Trust is the root of a successful relationship with your audience.

Telling your brand's story is like sharing your journey with a friend. People love to hear how you started, the struggles you faced, and the successes you achieved. For example, a handmade jewelry brand might share stories about how they learned their craft and the inspiration behind each piece. These stories make your brand more relatable and memorable. They create an emotional connection with your audience.

Building partnerships is like teaming up with a group of friends for a project. When you work together, you can achieve more than you could on your own. For example, a local coffee shop might collaborate with a bakery to offer a special deal for customers. These partnerships help expand your reach and bring more value to your audience. Working with others can make your brand stronger and more visible.

Your brand's reputation is like a mirror that reflects what people think about you. It is built over time through your actions and how you treat your customers. For example, providing excellent customer service and high-quality products helps create a positive reputation. A good reputation attracts more customers and keeps your existing ones loyal. Protecting your reputation is essential for long-term success.

Listening to feedback is like having a conversation with your audience. It helps you understand their needs and improve your brand. For example, if customers say they want more product options, you can work on expanding your offerings. Listening shows that you value their opinions and care about their satisfaction. This strengthens the bond between your brand and your audience.

Adapting to change is like adjusting your sails when the wind shifts. The business world is always evolving, and your brand needs to keep up. For example, if a new social media platform becomes popular, you should learn how to use it to connect with your audience. Staying flexible and open to change helps your brand stay relevant. It shows your audience that you are willing to grow and improve.

Investing in quality is like building a strong bridge that can hold heavy traffic. High-quality products and services create a good impression and keep customers coming back. For example, a clothing brand that uses durable materials and excellent craftsmanship will earn customer loyalty. Quality is something people remember and appreciate, and it sets your brand apart. It is a foundation for long-term success.

Your brand's values are like the roots of a tree. They keep you grounded and remind you of what is important. For example, if your brand values sustainability, those values should guide all your decisions, from product design to packaging. When your actions align with your values, it builds trust and respect with your audience. These values become a core part of your identity.

Storytelling in marketing is like painting a picture with words. It allows you to communicate your brand's message in a way that is engaging and memorable. For example, a travel company might share stories of real people's adventures to inspire others to explore the world. Stories create an emotional connection that facts alone cannot achieve. They make your brand more human and relatable.

Your brand's personality is like the character in a story. It gives your brand a unique voice and makes it easier for people to connect with you. For example, a tech company might have a friendly and innovative personality, while a luxury brand might be elegant and sophisticated. Your personality should match your audience's expectations and preferences. A strong personality helps your brand stand out in a crowded market.

Building a community around your brand is like hosting a gathering where everyone feels welcome. When people feel connected to your brand, they are more likely to stay loyal and spread the word. For example, creating a Facebook group or organizing local events can help bring your audience together. A strong community creates a sense of belonging and makes your brand more than just a business. It becomes a part of people's lives.

Your brand's visual identity is like a flag that represents who you are. It includes your logo, colors, fonts, and overall design. For example, a fitness brand might use bold colors and dynamic graphics to show energy and strength. A consistent visual identity helps people recognize your brand instantly. It is a powerful tool for creating a memorable and professional image.

Building your brand from scratch is a journey, not a race. It requires time, effort, and patience to create something meaningful. For example, starting small and focusing on getting the basics right can set you up for long-term success. Rushing the process can lead to mistakes and missed opportunities. Taking it step by step ensures that every part of your brand is strong and ready for growth.

Chapter 3: Crafting Content That Truly Connects

Crafting content that truly connects is like writing a heartfelt letter to someone you care about. You are not just sharing information; you are showing emotion, understanding, and thoughtfulness. The goal is to make your audience feel seen and heard, just like a letter would make someone feel special. For example, a post that acknowledges your audience's struggles with humor or sympathy shows them you relate to their experiences. This emotional connection is what makes your content stand out and resonate deeply with people.

Creating content starts with knowing your audience, like choosing the right gift for a friend. You would not give a book to someone who does not enjoy reading, just as you would not create content that your audience does not care about. For example, if your audience loves travel, sharing personal stories of adventures will catch their attention more than general updates. Understanding their likes, dislikes, and needs helps you create content that feels personal to them. When your content feels like a well-thought-out gift, people are more likely to appreciate and engage with it.

Your content is like a storybook, with each post being a chapter. A good story has a beginning, middle, and end, and it keeps the reader interested until the very last page. For example, a fitness coach might share a transformation journey, starting with struggles, showing progress, and ending with success. Each post builds on the last, encouraging the audience to keep following along. This type of storytelling keeps people invested in your content and excited for what comes next.

Visual content is like the clothing your message wears. Just as people notice how someone is dressed before starting a conversation, they notice visuals first in your posts. Bright colors, clean designs, or eye-catching photos can make your content hard to ignore. For example, a food blogger might use high-quality pictures of dishes to attract attention, even before the audience reads the recipe. When your visuals are appealing, they invite people to stop and engage with your message.

Using the right tone in your content is like using the right spices in a dish. Too much or too little can ruin the experience, but the right balance can make it perfect. For example, a playful tone might work well for a children's toy brand but feel out of place for financial services. Matching your tone to your audience and the message you want to share creates harmony. This makes your content feel natural and easy to connect with.

Good content is like a bridge that connects your brand to your audience. It helps you meet them where they are and guides them to where you want them to go. For example, an educational post about a product's benefits helps the audience understand why it is valuable. This bridge of information and connection builds trust and encourages people to take action. Without it, there is a gap that makes it harder to form relationships with your audience.

Engaging content is like hosting a lively conversation at a dinner party. You do not want to talk endlessly about yourself—you want to ask questions, listen, and respond. For example, a post that encourages followers to share their opinions or experiences invites interaction. This back-and-forth exchange makes your audience feel like they are part of something bigger. When you treat your content as a conversation, it becomes more dynamic and engaging.

Consistency in your content is like the rhythm in a song. Without a steady beat, the song feels unorganized and difficult to follow. Posting regularly and maintaining a consistent style ensures that your audience knows what to expect from you. For example, sharing tips every Tuesday or posting inspiring quotes every Friday creates a rhythm that keeps people coming back. This steady flow builds familiarity and trust with your audience.

Content that educates is like giving someone a map to navigate a new place. It provides them with the tools and knowledge they need to achieve their goals or solve their problems. For example, a skincare brand might share tips on how to create a daily routine for healthy skin. This type of content not only adds value but also positions your brand as a helpful and trustworthy expert. When people learn from you, they are more likely to remember and trust you.

Inspirational content is like a spark that lights a fire within. It motivates people to take action, try something new, or believe in themselves. For example, a fitness trainer might share before-and-after photos of clients to inspire others to start their own journey. This type of content taps into emotions and encourages people to dream big. When your content inspires, it creates a lasting impact that goes beyond simple engagement.

Content that entertains is like giving your audience a reason to smile after a long day. It provides a break from their routine and adds a little joy to their lives. For example, a pet brand might share funny videos of animals doing silly things that brighten people's moods. Entertainment builds a positive association with your brand and makes your content more shareable. When people laugh or feel happy because of your content, they are more likely to remember you.

Using metaphors in your content is like adding color to a black-and-white painting. Metaphors make ideas more relatable and easier to understand, giving your message depth and personality. For example, comparing a product to a superhero that saves the day helps people see its value in a creative way. Metaphors turn simple concepts into memorable and impactful messages. They make your content more enjoyable to read and share.

Interactive content is like inviting your audience to join you on stage during a performance. It makes them active participants instead of passive viewers. For example, a quiz about "Which travel destination suits your personality?" invites people to engage directly with your brand. This type of content keeps the experience fun and memorable, encouraging shares and discussions. When people participate, they feel more connected to your brand.

Sharing behind-the-scenes content is like giving your audience a backstage pass. It shows them the real, unpolished side of your brand, making it feel more human and authentic. For example, a bakery might share photos of the team preparing cakes or testing new recipes. This transparency builds trust and helps your audience feel like they are part of your journey. People appreciate honesty and love seeing the effort that goes into creating what they enjoy.

Reusing and repurposing content is like giving a new life to an old favorite song. Just as a remix can make an old track feel fresh again, reusing content in different formats keeps it relevant. For example, a blog post can be turned into a series of social media posts or an infographic. This strategy saves time and ensures that your message reaches more people in different ways. Repurposed content helps you get the most value out of your efforts.

Content that tells a personal story is like sharing a piece of your heart. It creates a deep emotional connection by showing vulnerability and authenticity. For example, a small business owner might share the challenges they faced when starting their company and how they overcame them. These personal stories inspire empathy and make your brand more relatable. When people see the human side of your brand, they feel closer to it.

Humor in content is like a good joke that brightens the mood at a party. It makes your audience smile, laugh, and feel good about interacting with your brand. For example, a coffee shop might share a funny meme about needing caffeine on a Monday morning. Humor adds personality to your content and makes it more shareable. However, it is important to use humor that aligns with your brand and audience.

Listening to your audience is like tuning into a radio station to hear what is playing. When you pay attention to their feedback, questions, and preferences, you can create content that truly resonates. For example, if many people ask for tips on a specific topic, you can create a post or video addressing that need. Listening shows your audience that you care about their opinions and are willing to adapt. This creates a stronger connection and encourages loyalty.

Testing different types of content is like exploring new recipes in the kitchen. You might not know what works best until you try a few different things and see what your audience enjoys the most. For example, experimenting with videos, infographics, and text-based posts can reveal what gets the most engagement. Testing helps you refine your approach and deliver content that truly resonates. It is a process of learning and improving over time.

Collaborating on content is like playing a duet with another musician. Two voices coming together can create something more powerful and engaging than one alone. For example, partnering with an influencer to create a post or video can introduce your brand to a new audience. Collaboration adds variety to your content and brings fresh perspectives. It shows your audience that you are open to new ideas and partnerships.

Timing your content is like planting seeds in the right season. Posting at the right time ensures that your audience is online and ready to engage. For example, a restaurant might post about dinner specials in the late afternoon when people are thinking about their evening plans. Timing increases the chances of your content being seen and acted upon. It helps you make the most out of your efforts.

Content that highlights your audience's achievements is like giving them a standing ovation. It celebrates their successes and makes them feel valued and appreciated. For example, a fitness brand might share stories and photos of customers reaching their fitness goals. This type of content builds a sense of community and encourages loyalty. When people feel celebrated, they are more likely to stay connected with your brand.

Adapting your content to trends is like joining a popular dance at a party. It shows that you are in tune with what is happening and willing to participate in the moment. For example, creating content around a viral hashtag or event can help you reach a wider audience. Adapting does not mean losing your brand's identity, but rather finding ways to stay relevant. It keeps your content fresh and engaging.

Crafting content that truly connects is an ongoing journey, like learning to play an instrument. It takes practice, patience, and the willingness to learn from your successes and mistakes. Each piece of content is an opportunity to improve and deepen your connection with your audience. By focusing on authenticity, creativity, and engagement, you can create content that leaves a lasting impact.

Chapter 4: Mastering Platforms for Maximum Impact

Mastering social media platforms for maximum impact is like learning how to use different types of tools in a workshop. Each tool has a specific purpose, and you need to understand how and when to use it. For example, Instagram is great for sharing visually appealing images, while LinkedIn is best for professional networking and industry news. Knowing the strengths of each platform allows you to use them effectively according to your goals. When you choose the right tool for the job, the results are always better.

Each social media platform is like a stage, and your content is the performance. On some stages, the audience prefers drama, while on others, they love comedy or music. For example, TikTok is a stage for short, creative videos, while Twitter is a stage for quick, witty thoughts. Understanding what type of content works best on each platform helps you deliver what the audience expects. This makes your performance memorable and keeps people coming back for more.

Using social media platforms is like speaking different languages to connect with people from different countries. Each platform has its own tone, style, and way of communicating with the audience. For example, Facebook users often prefer detailed posts and storytelling, while Instagram users enjoy attractive visuals with short captions. If you tailor your communication to match the platform's language, your message will resonate better. Speaking the right language helps you build stronger connections with your audience.

Consistency across platforms is like wearing a uniform that represents your team. It helps people recognize you no matter where they see you. For example, using the same logo, colors, and tone of voice on Instagram, Facebook, and LinkedIn makes your brand easily identifiable. This uniformity builds trust and familiarity, making it easier for your audience to remember you. When people see a consistent brand, they feel more confident in engaging with it.

Engaging with your audience on each platform is like hosting different kinds of parties. Some platforms are like casual get-togethers, where you can have light and fun conversations, while others are like formal events requiring more serious discussions. For example, Instagram could be your casual gathering where you share fun behind-the-scenes moments, while LinkedIn is your formal event for sharing in-depth industry insights. Hosting the right type of party on each platform ensures that your audience feels comfortable and engaged. When people enjoy the party, they are more likely to stay and interact.

Understanding platform algorithms is like learning the rules of a game. If you do not know how the game works, you might keep losing no matter how hard you try. For example, Instagram's algorithm favors consistent posting and engagement, while TikTok rewards creative and trending content. By learning the rules, you can adjust your strategies to improve your chances of success. Mastering the game increases your visibility and helps you reach more people.

Posting at the right time on each platform is like planting seeds during the right season. If you plant too early or too late, the seeds might not grow. For example, posting on Twitter in the morning might catch the attention of people commuting to work, while posting on Instagram in the evening might reach people relaxing after their day. Timing your posts ensures that your audience is online and ready to engage. When the timing is right, your content has a better chance of making an impact.

The hashtags you use on platforms are like signposts on a busy road. They guide people to your content and help them find what they are looking for. For example, using hashtags like #TravelTips or #HealthyRecipes makes it easier for people interested in those topics to discover your posts. Signposts make navigating the road simpler and more effective for everyone. When your hashtags are clear and relevant, they bring the right audience to your content.

Collaborating with influencers on platforms is like partnering with a tour guide who knows the area well. Influencers already have an established audience that trusts them, and they can introduce your brand to their followers. For example, a skincare brand might work with a beauty influencer to showcase their products in tutorials or reviews. This partnership helps you reach new audiences and build credibility. A good tour guide makes the journey smoother and more enjoyable.

Paid advertisements on platforms are like billboards on a busy highway. They catch the attention of people passing by and encourage them to take action. For example, running an ad on Facebook to promote a sale can bring in more customers who might not have found you otherwise. Billboards are a way to stand out in a crowded space and deliver your message effectively. When used wisely, paid ads can help you reach your goals faster.

Analyzing your performance on platforms is like checking the scoreboard during a game. It shows you what is working and what needs improvement. For example, if a specific type of post gets more likes and comments, you can focus on creating similar content. The scoreboard provides valuable insights that guide your next moves. By paying attention to the numbers, you can make better decisions and improve your strategy.

Adapting to updates on platforms is like upgrading your tools to handle new challenges. Social media platforms often change their features or algorithms, and staying updated helps you stay ahead. For example, when Instagram introduced reels, many brands quickly adapted by creating short, engaging videos. Upgrading your tools ensures that you can continue to perform well in a changing environment. Being flexible and willing to adapt is key to long-term success.

Building a community on platforms is like creating a neighborhood where people feel welcome and connected. It is not just about sharing content but also about fostering relationships and conversations. For example, a fitness brand might create a Facebook group where followers can share their progress, ask questions, and motivate each other. A strong community encourages loyalty and makes your audience feel valued. When people feel like they belong, they are more likely to support your brand.

Using platform-specific features is like using the special functions on a gadget to make your work easier. Each platform offers unique tools that can enhance your content and engagement. For example, Instagram Stories and polls allow you to interact with your audience in fun and creative ways. Taking advantage of these features helps you stand out and keeps your content fresh. When you use all the tools available, you maximize your potential impact.

Your profile on each platform is like the front door to your home. It is the first thing people see, and it should invite them in. For example, a clear and engaging bio with a professional profile picture can make a great first impression on LinkedIn. Your profile should clearly communicate who you are and what you offer. When your front door is welcoming, more people will want to step inside.

Cross-promoting your content on platforms is like setting up signs pointing to different parts of a park. Each sign directs visitors to another exciting area they might enjoy. For example, you can share a snippet of a YouTube video on Instagram and encourage followers to watch the full video. These signs help guide your audience to explore more of your content. Cross-promotion increases visibility and keeps people engaged with your brand.

Building trust on platforms is like laying bricks one by one to construct a sturdy wall. Each interaction, post, or comment adds another brick to the wall of trust. For example, responding to comments and messages promptly shows that you value your audience. Over time, this consistency builds a strong foundation of trust and loyalty. A sturdy wall takes time to build, but it provides long-lasting support.

Understanding your competitors on platforms is like studying your opponents before a match. Knowing their strengths and weaknesses helps you create a better strategy. For example, if you notice that a competitor gets a lot of engagement with video content, you can focus on creating your own high-quality videos.

Studying others helps you learn and improve your own approach. It gives you an edge in a competitive environment.

Planning your content for platforms is like packing for a trip. You need to prepare everything in advance to ensure a smooth journey. For example, creating a content calendar helps you stay organized and consistent with your posts. When you have a clear plan, it reduces stress and allows you to focus on creativity. A well-packed bag ensures that you are ready for anything that comes your way.

Engaging with trends on platforms is like joining a popular dance at a party. It shows that you are aware of what is happening and willing to participate in the fun. For example, using trending hashtags or creating content around viral challenges can help you reach a wider audience. Joining the dance helps you stay relevant and connect with more people. Trends are an opportunity to showcase your creativity and adaptability.

Using analytics on platforms is like having a compass to guide your journey. It points you in the right direction and helps you avoid getting lost. For example, tracking which posts perform best can help you understand what your audience enjoys most. This information allows you to refine your strategy and focus on what works. A good compass ensures that you are always moving closer to your goals.

Chapter 5: Growing Audiences with Proven Strategies

Growing an audience with proven strategies is like planting a garden. It requires patience, care, and the right methods to see growth over time. You cannot just throw seeds anywhere and expect them to grow; they need attention and nurturing. For example, posting quality content regularly is like watering your plants to keep them healthy. When you invest time and effort, your audience will grow just like a well-cared-for garden.

Knowing your audience is like choosing the right seeds to plant in your garden. Different plants need different soil, sunlight, and water, just as different audiences have unique needs and preferences. For example, if your audience enjoys educational content, creating how-to videos or tutorials will resonate with them. If you plant the wrong seeds, they will not grow, and similarly, if you create content that does not match your audience's interests, they will not engage. Understanding your audience helps you lay the foundation for successful growth.

Creating shareable content is like creating a recipe that everyone wants to share with their friends. When people find something valuable or entertaining, they naturally want to pass it on. For example, a funny meme or an inspiring story can quickly go viral if it resonates with your audience. This sharing spreads your content to new people who might not have discovered you otherwise. Just like a good recipe, shareable content multiplies your efforts and reaches a wider audience.

Using social media platforms effectively is like planting in the right environment for your plants. Some plants grow well in sunny areas, while others prefer shade, just as some types of content work better on certain platforms. For example, visually appealing content thrives on Instagram, while short, informative posts perform well on Twitter. Knowing the best place to post your content ensures it reaches the right audience. When you plant in the right environment, your chances of success increase.

Consistency in posting is like keeping a steady rhythm in a song. If the rhythm is irregular, the song loses its flow, just as inconsistent posting confuses your audience. For example, if you post every Monday and Thursday, your audience will know when to expect new content. This regularity builds trust and keeps your audience engaged over time. A steady rhythm creates harmony and keeps everything moving smoothly.

Engaging with your audience is like having a conversation at a dinner table. You do not want to do all the talking; you also want to listen and respond. For example, replying to comments, answering questions, and asking for feedback shows your audience that you value their input. This interaction creates a sense of community and makes people feel connected to your brand. A good conversation makes people want to stay and participate.

Running contests and giveaways is like throwing a party to attract more people to your event. Everyone loves the chance to win something, and these activities generate excitement and interest. For example, you might ask followers to tag their friends or share your post to enter a giveaway. This not only engages your current audience but also introduces your brand to new people. A fun party always leaves a positive impression and brings more guests.

Collaborating with influencers is like teaming up with a popular guide who knows the area well. Influencers have an established audience that trusts their opinions, and they can introduce your brand to their followers. For example, a fitness influencer promoting your workout gear can bring your products to people who are already interested in fitness. This collaboration helps you reach a larger audience and build credibility. A trusted guide makes exploring new areas easier and more effective.

Using analytics to track your progress is like checking a map to make sure you are on the right path. Without it, you might keep going in circles without realizing it. For example, analyzing which posts get the most likes or shares helps you understand what your audience enjoys. This allows you to focus on creating more of that type of content. A good map helps you navigate your journey successfully.

Encouraging user-generated content is like letting your audience plant their own seeds in your garden. When people share their experiences with your brand, it adds authenticity and creates a ripple effect. For example, a customer posting a photo of themselves wearing your product can inspire others to do the same. This type of content builds trust and expands your reach through word of mouth. When everyone participates, the garden becomes richer and more vibrant.

Storytelling in your content is like painting a picture that captures attention and emotions. A good story draws people in, makes them feel something, and leaves a lasting impression. For example, sharing how your brand started or the challenges you overcame can inspire and connect with your audience. These personal touches make your brand more relatable and memorable. A beautiful picture stays in the mind long after it is seen.

Using hashtags effectively is like putting up signs that guide people to your garden. Hashtags help people discover your content when they are looking for something specific. For example, using hashtags like #FitnessGoals or #TravelTips can bring more visibility to your posts. Clear and relevant signs make it easier for people to find what they are searching for. When you use hashtags wisely, your audience grows naturally.

Offering valuable content is like giving your audience a gift they can use. People appreciate content that solves their problems, answers their questions, or entertains them. For example, a cooking blog sharing easy recipes for busy families provides value to its audience. When people feel they are getting something useful, they are more likely to stay loyal to your brand. A thoughtful gift always leaves a good impression.

Building a community around your brand is like creating a neighborhood where everyone supports each other. A strong community keeps people coming back and encourages them to invite others. For example, a fitness app might create an online group where users can share their progress and motivate each other. This sense of belonging makes your audience more engaged and loyal. A welcoming neighborhood is one where people love to spend time.

Using email marketing is like sending a personal invitation to your audience. Emails allow you to connect directly with your followers and keep them updated. For example, a monthly newsletter can share tips, updates, and special offers with your subscribers. This direct communication builds a closer relationship with your audience. A personal invitation always feels special and appreciated.

Experimenting with different types of content is like trying out new recipes in the kitchen. You might not know what your audience loves most until you try a variety of options. For example, testing videos, infographics, or blog posts can reveal what gets the most engagement. Experimenting allows you to discover what works best and keeps your content fresh. A good chef always tries new things to improve their menu.

Adapting to trends is like adjusting your sails to catch the wind. Trends can give your content a boost by making it more timely and relevant. For example, participating in a viral challenge or using a trending hashtag can help you reach a wider audience. Catching the wind at the right time helps you move forward faster. Staying flexible and open to change keeps you ahead of the competition.

Encouraging reviews and testimonials is like collecting happy stories from people who have visited your garden. Positive reviews build trust and attract new people who want to experience the same. For example, showcasing customer testimonials on your website or social media can highlight the value of your brand. These stories act as proof that your brand delivers on its promises. Happy visitors always bring more friends along.

Investing in paid ads is like putting up billboards to attract more attention to your garden. Ads help you reach people who might not have found you otherwise. For example, running a Facebook or Instagram ad campaign can bring in new followers and customers. A well-placed billboard catches the eye and inspires action. When used wisely, paid ads can speed up your audience growth.

Using video content is like giving your audience a front-row seat to a live performance. Videos are engaging, dynamic, and allow you to share your message in a more personal way. For example, a behind-the-scenes video of your team working on a project can humanize your brand. This type of content keeps people interested and coming back for more. A great performance always leaves the audience wanting more.

Sharing milestones and achievements is like celebrating the growth of your garden with your visitors. It shows your audience how far you have come and makes them feel part of your journey. For example, posting about reaching a follower milestone or launching a new product creates excitement and gratitude. Celebrations make people feel included and appreciated. A shared moment of joy strengthens the connection between you and your audience.

Partnering with complementary brands is like combining two gardens to create a bigger and more beautiful space. Working together allows you to reach new audiences while offering more value to your followers. For example, a coffee shop might partner with a bakery to promote each other's products. This collaboration benefits both brands and their audiences. A combined effort always creates something greater.

Remaining patient is like waiting for your garden to bloom. Growing an audience takes time, and results do not happen overnight. For example, it might take months of consistent posts and engagement before you see significant growth. Patience and persistence are essential for long-term success. A beautiful garden is worth the wait.

Chapter 6: Engaging Followers and Sparking Conversations

Engaging followers and sparking conversations is like starting a campfire. At first, you need small sparks to get it going, but once the flames catch, the fire grows and warms everyone around it. On social media, these sparks could be a question or a relatable post that invites people to share their thoughts. For example, asking your audience, "What is your favorite way to relax after a long day?" can encourage them to comment and interact. When the fire of conversation starts, it creates a warm and welcoming space for everyone.

Talking to your followers online is like chatting with friends at a coffee shop. It is important to listen as much as you talk and make the conversation enjoyable for everyone. For example, when someone comments on your post, take the time to reply with a thoughtful response. This shows that you value their opinion and care about what they have to say. A friendly chat builds stronger connections and keeps people coming back for more.

Asking open-ended questions in your posts is like opening a door for others to walk through. Questions like "What are your thoughts on this topic?" or "What would you do in this situation?" invite people to share their opinions and stories. For example, a travel company might ask, "What is your dream destination and why?" This encourages followers to share their dreams and experiences, sparking meaningful conversations. Leaving the door open for dialogue makes your audience feel welcome and included.

Sharing relatable content is like telling a joke or story that everyone understands. It makes people nod their heads and say, "That is so true!" For example, a post about the Monday blues or the joy of finding an extra fry in your meal can connect with people emotionally. Relatable moments remind your audience that you understand their lives and experiences. When people feel understood, they are more likely to respond and engage.

Using visuals in your posts is like adding pictures to a storybook. A story without pictures can be interesting, but adding visuals makes it more engaging and easier to connect with. For example, a motivational quote with a beautiful sunset background can capture attention and inspire your audience. Images and videos give your content more depth and make it stand out in a sea of words. A colorful and dynamic storybook always attracts more readers.

Replying to comments is like saying thank you after receiving a gift. When someone takes the time to comment on your post, it is important to acknowledge their effort. For example, if a follower shares how much they love your product, replying with "Thank you so much! We are so glad you like it!" shows appreciation. This small gesture makes people feel valued and encourages them to interact more in the future. Gratitude strengthens relationships and keeps the conversation alive.

Creating polls and surveys is like passing around a clipboard at a meeting to gather everyone's input. It gives your audience a chance to share their preferences and opinions in a quick and easy way. For example, a clothing brand might ask, "Which color do you prefer for our next collection: blue or green?" This not only sparks engagement but also helps you learn more about what your audience wants. When people feel heard, they are more likely to stay connected to your brand.

Using humor in your posts is like making people laugh at a party. A good laugh breaks the ice and brings people closer together. For example, a funny meme about the struggles of waking up early can resonate with many people and encourage them to comment or share. Humor creates a happy and relaxed atmosphere where conversations can flourish. A smile is often the first step toward connection.

Highlighting your followers is like giving someone a moment to shine on stage. Sharing their stories, photos, or testimonials shows that you appreciate their support and value their contributions. For example, a fitness brand might repost a follower's progress photo and congratulate them on their journey. This not only makes the featured person feel special but also inspires others to join the conversation. Giving the spotlight to your audience strengthens your community and deepens engagement.

Hosting live sessions is like inviting your audience to a real-time discussion in your living room. It creates a sense of closeness and allows for spontaneous conversations. For example, a chef might host a live cooking session where followers can ask questions and share their own tips. This interactive experience makes your audience feel like they are part of the moment. Live sessions create a unique opportunity for connection that pre-recorded content cannot match.

Encouraging user-generated content is like inviting your audience to help decorate your space. When followers create and share content related to your brand, it adds authenticity and variety to your presence. For example, a travel agency might ask followers to share their favorite vacation photos with a specific hashtag. This sparks conversations and builds a sense of collaboration between you and your audience. Decorating together makes the space feel more personal and inviting.

Sharing behind-the-scenes content is like showing people what happens backstage at a theater. It reveals the effort, creativity, and teamwork behind your brand, making it feel more real and relatable. For example, a bakery might share videos of their staff preparing fresh bread early in the morning. This transparency invites followers to connect with your brand on a deeper level. A peek behind the curtain often sparks curiosity and engagement.

Using stories in your posts is like sitting around a campfire and sharing tales. Stories capture attention, evoke emotions, and encourage people to share their own experiences. For example, a small business owner might post about how they started their business and the challenges they faced along the way. These personal stories inspire empathy and make your brand more memorable. When people connect with your story, they are more likely to continue the conversation.

Hosting challenges is like organizing a friendly competition at a community event. Challenges encourage participation and create excitement among your followers. For example, a fitness brand might run a "30-day workout challenge" and invite followers to share their progress. This not only sparks conversations but also builds a sense of camaraderie among participants. A little competition adds energy and fun to your interactions.

Collaborating with influencers is like introducing a friend to a new group of people. Influencers can help you reach a larger audience and start conversations with people who trust their opinions. For example, a beauty brand might partner with a makeup artist to demonstrate their products in tutorials. This collaboration introduces your brand to new followers and encourages them to engage. A trusted introduction often leads to meaningful connections.

Hosting Q&A sessions is like opening the floor for questions at the end of a presentation. It gives your audience a chance to ask what they want to know and feel more involved. For example, a tech company might invite followers to ask questions about their latest product launch. Answering these questions shows that you are approachable and willing to help. A good Q&A session sparks curiosity and builds trust.

Using emojis in your posts is like adding facial expressions to your words. They add emotion and personality to your content, making it more relatable and fun. For example, using a laughing emoji in a humorous post or a heart emoji in a thankful message can enhance the tone of your content. Emojis help your audience understand the mood and intention behind your words. A little emotion goes a long way in creating connection.

Encouraging conversations about current topics is like joining a discussion at a town square. Addressing relevant issues or trends shows that you are engaged with what is happening in the world. For example, a sustainable brand might start a conversation about reducing plastic waste and invite followers to share their ideas. This not only sparks meaningful discussions but also positions your brand as socially aware. A timely and thoughtful discussion brings people together and builds trust.

Responding to direct messages is like having one-on-one conversations in a quiet corner. It creates a personal connection and shows that you value individual interactions. For example, a customer might send a message asking about product recommendations, and your thoughtful response can turn them into a loyal supporter. These private conversations build trust and deepen relationships. A personal touch always makes a big difference.

Using call-to-action phrases in your posts is like giving clear directions to a group of people. Phrases like "Share your story in the comments" or "Tag a friend who needs this" encourage followers to take specific actions. For example, a motivational post might end with "Tell us what inspires you today!" This invites participation and keeps the conversation going. Clear directions make it easier for people to engage.

Sharing tips and advice is like offering helpful tools to someone working on a project. It provides value and positions your brand as a knowledgeable and trustworthy source. For example, a skincare brand might share tips on how to keep skin hydrated during winter. When people find your content helpful, they are more likely to interact and return for more. Offering useful tools builds loyalty and sparks gratitude.

Highlighting common interests is like finding shared hobbies with a new friend. When you talk about topics your audience cares about, it creates a natural connection. For example, a pet brand might post about the joys and challenges of being a pet owner, sparking conversations among animal lovers. These shared interests make your audience feel like they are part of a community. Finding common ground is the foundation of meaningful engagement.

Encouraging positivity in your posts is like spreading sunshine on a cloudy day. Positive messages lift people's spirits and create a welcoming environment for interaction. For example, a motivational post about overcoming challenges can inspire followers to share their own experiences. Positivity attracts engagement and builds a supportive community around your brand. A little sunshine can brighten everyone's day.

Engaging followers and sparking conversations is an ongoing process, like tending to a fire to keep it burning. It requires consistent effort, care, and creativity to maintain the warmth and energy. Every comment, reply, or post is an opportunity to deepen connections and build trust with your audience. When you keep the flames alive, your community grows stronger and more vibrant over time. A well-tended fire brings people together and keeps them coming back for more.

Chapter 7: Analyzing Data to Drive Results

Analyzing data to drive results is like using a compass during a hike. Without it, you might wander aimlessly, unsure of which direction to take. Data acts as your guide, helping you understand where you are and where you need to go. For example, looking at your social media engagement numbers can show you which posts your audience enjoys the most. Like a compass, this insight helps you stay on the right path toward your goals.

Collecting data is like gathering ingredients for a recipe. You need the right mix to create something successful. For example, you might track likes, comments, and shares on social media to understand how well your content is performing. Each piece of data is like an ingredient that contributes to the overall picture. Without the right ingredients, the final result may not turn out as expected.

Understanding your audience through data is like listening to a friend tell you what they like and dislike. When you pay attention, you learn what makes them happy and what does not. For instance, if your data shows that posts with images get more engagement than text-only posts, you know to focus more on visuals. This understanding helps you create content that truly connects with your audience. Listening carefully allows you to build stronger relationships.

Tracking trends in your data is like watching the weather to plan your day. If you notice it is getting colder, you know to wear a jacket. Similarly, if you see a rise in engagement during certain days or times, you can adjust your posting schedule. For example, if your audience is most active in the evening, posting during that time can maximize your reach. Watching the trends helps you prepare and make better decisions.

Analyzing data over time is like watching a plant grow. You cannot see big changes from one day to the next, but over weeks and months, growth becomes clear. For example, tracking your follower count monthly can show steady increases or sudden drops. This long-term view helps you understand the bigger picture of your progress. Monitoring growth allows you to celebrate successes and address challenges.

Identifying patterns in your data is like solving a puzzle. Each piece of information fits together to create a clearer picture. For example, if you notice that product posts perform better than general updates, you can focus more on promoting your products. These patterns help you understand what works and what does not. Solving the puzzle allows you to improve your strategy.

Using data to improve your strategy is like fixing a broken machine. If something is not working, data shows you where the problem is so you can make adjustments. For instance, if your ads are not getting clicks, analyzing the data can reveal whether the issue is with the design, the message, or the audience targeting. By making changes based on the data, you can get the machine running smoothly again. Fixing the problem ensures better results in the future.

Comparing data from different campaigns is like trying on different outfits to see which one looks best. Each campaign has its own style, and data helps you decide which approach works better. For example, if one ad brings in more sales than another, you know which style to repeat. This comparison helps you refine your marketing efforts. Trying different options allows you to find the perfect fit for your audience.

Setting goals based on data is like setting checkpoints on a long journey. These checkpoints help you measure progress and stay motivated. For example, if your data shows you are gaining 100 new followers a month, you can set a goal to reach 1,000 followers in ten months. Data-driven goals keep you focused and give you something to strive for. Reaching each checkpoint brings you closer to your destination.

Using data to spot opportunities is like finding hidden treasures on a map. Sometimes, the numbers reveal possibilities you had not considered before. For instance, if data shows that a specific age group engages most with your content, you can create more targeted posts for them. These opportunities help you expand your reach and improve your results. Discovering hidden treasures can lead to unexpected success.

Analyzing competitors' data is like watching how other players perform in a game. It helps you understand their strengths and weaknesses so you can improve your own strategy. For example, if a competitor gets more engagement by using videos, you might decide to create more video content too. Learning from others allows you to grow and stay competitive. Observing the game helps you play smarter.

Using visuals to interpret data is like translating a foreign language into something you can understand. Charts, graphs, and infographics make complex numbers easier to read and analyze.

For example, a line graph showing your monthly sales growth is easier to understand than a long list of numbers. Visuals turn data into a story that is clear and actionable. A good translation makes communication smoother.

Testing ideas based on data is like experimenting with different recipes in the kitchen. You use what you have learned to create something new and see how it turns out. For example, if data shows that short videos perform well, you can test creating more of them to see if the trend continues. Experimenting allows you to find new ways to engage your audience. Each test brings you closer to the perfect recipe for success.

Filtering unnecessary data is like clearing out clutter from a messy room. Too much information can be overwhelming, so you need to focus on what is most important. For example, if your goal is to increase sales, tracking website traffic and conversion rates matters more than tracking likes on posts. Keeping the relevant data helps you stay organized and focused. A clear space makes it easier to see what truly matters.

Sharing data insights with your team is like sharing a map with fellow travelers. When everyone understands the direction, they can work together more effectively. For example, showing your team which types of posts perform best can guide their future content creation. Sharing this information ensures everyone is aligned and working toward the same goals. A shared map keeps everyone on track.

Using data to predict future trends is like reading the stars to navigate the seas. It helps you anticipate what lies ahead and prepare for it. For example, if your data shows a consistent rise in video engagement, you can focus more on video content for future campaigns. Predictions based on data give you an advantage in planning your next moves. Navigating with foresight leads to smoother sailing.

Learning from past mistakes through data is like studying a playbook after losing a game. It helps you see what went wrong and how you can do better next time. For example, if a campaign did not perform well, analyzing the data can reveal whether the issue was timing, content, or audience targeting. These lessons allow you to avoid repeating the same mistakes. A careful review of the playbook can turn losses into wins.

Tracking return on investment is like measuring the harvest after planting seeds. You want to know if the effort and resources you put in were worth it. For example, comparing the money spent on ads to the sales generated shows whether your investment paid off. This measurement helps you decide where to focus your budget in the future. A bountiful harvest proves that your efforts were successful.

Automating data analysis is like using a machine to sort through a pile of papers. It saves time and ensures accuracy, allowing you to focus on making decisions. For example, using tools that automatically track website traffic and engagement rates can simplify your work. Automation helps you stay organized and efficient. A well-functioning machine makes the process smoother and faster.

Interpreting audience feedback through data is like reading the reviews of a book. It shows you what people liked and what they did not, helping you improve your next release. For example, if your audience responds positively to interactive content, you can plan to create more quizzes or polls. Feedback provides valuable insights for refining your strategy. A good review makes it easier to create something even better next time.

Using data to personalize content is like tailoring a suit to fit perfectly. It ensures that your message matches the needs and preferences of your audience. For instance, if data shows that a segment of your audience prefers discounts, you can send them targeted offers. Personalization makes your audience feel valued and understood. A well-fitted suit always leaves a great impression.

Setting benchmarks with data is like setting milestones during a marathon. These markers help you measure your progress and stay motivated to reach the finish line. For example, tracking weekly engagement rates can show whether you are improving or need to adjust your strategy. Benchmarks give you a clear sense of direction and accomplishment. Each milestone brings you closer to achieving your goals.

Using data to showcase success is like displaying trophies after a competition. It proves your achievements and builds credibility with your audience. For example, sharing stats like "Our posts reached 10,000 people this month" shows your growth and impact. Highlighting these successes inspires confidence and attracts more followers. A well-earned trophy always gets noticed.

Chapter 8: Navigating Challenges and Adapting Fast

Navigating challenges and adapting fast is like steering a boat in a storm. When the waves are rough, you need to stay calm and adjust your direction to keep moving forward. Challenges on social media, like unexpected negative feedback or changing trends, can feel overwhelming at times. For example, if a campaign does not perform well, you might feel stuck, but making quick changes based on audience feedback can help you recover. Steering through the storm teaches you how to stay focused and find smoother waters.

Every challenge is like a puzzle waiting to be solved. It might look complicated at first, but if you analyze the pieces carefully, you can find a solution. For example, if your engagement suddenly drops, looking at the timing, content type, or audience behavior can help you pinpoint the issue. Each detail is a piece of the puzzle that contributes to the bigger picture. Solving the puzzle helps you understand the problem and take the right steps to fix it.

Adapting to change is like learning to dance to a new rhythm. When the music changes, you cannot keep dancing the same way. For example, if a new social media platform becomes popular, you need to learn how to use it to reach your audience. Adjusting your strategy allows you to stay relevant and connected. Just like a dancer, being flexible and responsive keeps you in sync with your environment.

Facing competition is like running a marathon with other runners. You do not need to focus on beating everyone; instead, you focus on running your best race. For example, if a competitor launches a successful campaign, you can study their approach and find ways to improve your own. Healthy competition pushes you to grow and find unique ways to stand out. Running your race with determination helps you achieve long-term success.

Handling negative feedback is like putting out a small fire before it spreads. Ignoring it can make things worse, but addressing it calmly can prevent further damage. For example, if a customer complains about your product on social media, responding politely and offering a solution shows that you care. This approach not only resolves the issue but also builds trust with your audience. Putting out the fire quickly keeps your reputation intact.

Learning from mistakes is like falling off a bicycle and getting back on. Every fall teaches you something new about balance and control. For example, if a post does not get the engagement you expected, you can analyze what went wrong and improve your next one. Mistakes are opportunities to grow and refine your strategies. Each time you get back on the bike, you become a better rider.

Staying calm under pressure is like being the captain of a ship during a storm. The crew looks to the captain for guidance, just as your team or audience looks to you for leadership. For example, if there is a sudden controversy involving your brand, staying calm and responding thoughtfully can prevent panic. A steady hand inspires confidence and helps everyone navigate the challenge together. Calmness is the anchor that keeps the ship steady.

Adapting your content is like changing the ingredients in a recipe based on what is available. Sometimes, you need to adjust your approach to suit the situation. For example, if your audience becomes more interested in video content, shifting your focus from photos to short videos can keep them engaged. Flexibility allows you to make the most of what you have. Like a good chef, adapting your recipe ensures that the final result is still satisfying.

Anticipating challenges is like reading the weather forecast before a trip. If you know a storm is coming, you can prepare and avoid surprises. For example, keeping an eye on social media trends and updates helps you adapt before your current strategy becomes outdated. Preparation makes it easier to handle changes smoothly. A good forecast helps you plan and stay ahead of the curve.

Turning challenges into opportunities is like finding a silver lining in a cloudy sky. Difficult situations often come with hidden benefits if you look closely. For example, if a campaign faces criticism, using the feedback to improve your future efforts can strengthen your connection with your audience. Challenges push you to think creatively and find new solutions. Each cloud has the potential to brighten your day in unexpected ways.

Collaborating with others during tough times is like having teammates to help you lift a heavy load. Sharing ideas and resources makes it easier to overcome obstacles. For example, partnering with influencers or other brands can help you reach a wider audience when your engagement is low. Collaboration brings fresh perspectives and shared support. A strong team makes even the heaviest load manageable.

Staying patient when facing challenges is like waiting for a seed to grow. Growth takes time, and rushing can lead to mistakes. For example, if your new content strategy does not show results immediately, giving it time to develop can reveal its true potential. Patience allows you to see the bigger picture and make informed decisions. Just like a plant, success blossoms with care and time.

Using data to overcome challenges is like using a flashlight in a dark tunnel. It helps you see what lies ahead and guides your next steps. For example, analyzing engagement metrics during a slow period can reveal what type of content your audience prefers. Data provides clarity and direction in uncertain times. A well-lit path makes the journey less intimidating.

Adapting to audience feedback is like adjusting the sails of a boat to catch the wind. Listening to your audience allows you to align with their needs and preferences. For example, if followers request more educational content, creating tutorials or how-to posts can strengthen your connection with them. Adjusting your sails keeps you moving forward efficiently. A responsive approach builds trust and loyalty.

Managing your resources during challenges is like rationing supplies on a long trip. You need to use what you have wisely to ensure it lasts. For example, focusing on high-impact content and campaigns during a budget constraint can help you achieve results without overspending. Efficient resource management keeps you moving forward despite limitations. Smart planning ensures you reach your destination without running out of fuel.

Celebrating small wins during challenges is like finding a resting spot on a long hike. It gives you a chance to recharge and appreciate your progress. For example, reaching a small milestone, like a slight increase in engagement, can motivate you to keep going. Acknowledging these moments reminds you that every step counts. A rest stop inspires you to continue your journey with renewed energy.

Keeping a positive attitude is like wearing a raincoat in the rain. It does not stop the rain, but it keeps you dry and comfortable. For example, viewing a drop in sales as an opportunity to rethink your strategy can help you stay motivated. Positivity helps you focus on solutions rather than problems. A sunny outlook makes even rainy days bearable.

Learning new skills during challenges is like sharpening your tools for future use. Each skill you gain prepares you for the next obstacle. For example, learning how to create video content during a shift in audience preferences can make you more versatile. These skills become valuable assets that strengthen your strategy. A well-equipped toolbox is essential for tackling any challenge.

Turning setbacks into lessons is like turning a detour into an adventure. While it might take you off your planned route, it can lead to new discoveries. For example, if a campaign fails, analyzing what went wrong can teach you how to avoid similar mistakes in the future. Every setback is an opportunity to grow and improve. A detour often leads to unexpected and valuable experiences.

Staying adaptable in a fast-changing world is like being a chameleon that blends into its environment. Flexibility allows you to adjust quickly and thrive in new situations. For example, when new social media features are introduced, learning how to use them effectively can give you an advantage. Adaptability ensures that you remain relevant and competitive. A chameleon's ability to change keeps it safe and successful.

Seeking advice from experts during challenges is like asking for directions when you are lost. Guidance from someone experienced can save you time and effort. For example, consulting with a marketing expert can help you identify solutions to a campaign problem. Expert advice provides clarity and confidence in difficult times. A good guide makes finding your way much easier.

Focusing on your long-term vision is like looking at the horizon while sailing. It reminds you of your ultimate destination even when the waters are rough. For example, staying committed to your brand's mission during temporary challenges helps you stay motivated and focused. A clear vision keeps you moving in the right direction. The horizon provides hope and purpose on the journey.

Navigating challenges and adapting fast is an ongoing journey, like climbing a mountain. Each step brings new obstacles, but also new opportunities to grow stronger and wiser. By staying flexible, calm, and focused, you can overcome any difficulty that comes your way. Every challenge teaches you something valuable and prepares you for the future. Reaching the top of the mountain is a reward worth all the effort.

Chapter 9: Sustaining Growth in Changing Times

Sustaining growth in changing times is like keeping a plant healthy as the seasons change. Sometimes the sun is shining, and other times the weather is rough, but with care and attention, the plant can keep growing. Your business or social media presence needs the same care to adapt and survive through changes. For example, when trends shift or platforms update their features, you need to adjust your approach to stay relevant. Just like a gardener, you must be flexible and ready to provide what your plant needs to thrive.

Consistency is like watering your plant at regular intervals. If you forget to water it or do it too much, the plant might wither. Similarly, in business, staying consistent with your content, messaging, and engagement is key to keeping your audience connected. For example, posting regularly on social media ensures that your brand stays visible and top of mind for your followers. A steady routine builds trust and shows your audience that you are reliable.

Adapting to changes is like adjusting the sails of a boat when the wind shifts. If you do not adjust, the boat will move in the wrong direction or stop altogether. For instance, when a new social media platform becomes popular, learning how to use it effectively can help you reach a new audience. Adapting quickly to these changes ensures that your growth does not stop. Changing your sails keeps your journey moving forward.

Building strong relationships with your audience is like creating deep roots for a tree. When the roots are strong, the tree can survive storms and continue to grow. For example, engaging with your audience through comments, messages, and helpful content builds loyalty and trust. This relationship creates a stable foundation that supports your brand even during difficult times. A tree with deep roots can weather any storm.

Diversifying your efforts is like planting different types of crops in your field. If one crop fails, you can still rely on the others to sustain you. For example, if you rely only on one social media platform for growth, you might face challenges if that platform changes its rules. Instead, spreading your efforts across multiple platforms or strategies helps you stay secure. A diverse field ensures that you always have something to fall back on.

Staying informed about changes in your industry is like checking the weather forecast before leaving the house. Knowing what is coming helps you prepare and make smart decisions. For example, if you know that video content is becoming more popular, you can start creating videos to stay ahead of the trend. Staying informed ensures that you are not caught off guard. A good forecast helps you navigate the future with confidence.

Investing in innovation is like upgrading your tools to make your work more efficient. New tools and ideas can help you do things better and reach your goals faster. For example, using analytics tools to track your performance can help you understand what is working and what needs improvement. Innovation keeps your approach fresh and relevant in a changing world. Upgraded tools make the job easier and more effective.

Listening to feedback from your audience is like checking the health of your plant by looking at its leaves. The leaves can tell you if the plant is getting enough water or sunlight. Similarly, your audience's feedback tells you if your content or product is meeting their needs. For example, if customers ask for more tutorials, creating helpful videos can strengthen your relationship with them. Paying attention to these signs helps you make adjustments and continue growing.

Setting long-term goals is like drawing a map for a long journey. The map keeps you focused on where you want to go, even if the path is not always clear. For example, if your goal is to reach 10,000 followers in a year, you can break it into smaller monthly targets. Having a clear map helps you measure your progress and stay motivated. A good map makes the journey more manageable and rewarding.

Celebrating small wins along the way is like stopping to enjoy the view during a hike. These moments remind you of how far you have come and give you energy to keep moving forward. For example, reaching a milestone like gaining 500 new followers or launching a successful campaign is worth celebrating. Acknowledging these achievements keeps your team and audience motivated. A beautiful view along the way makes the hike more enjoyable.

Staying flexible with your strategy is like being an artist who can switch between brushes and tools. Different situations require different approaches, and being able to adapt makes you more effective. For instance, if an ad campaign is not performing well, testing a new design or message can improve its success. Flexibility allows you to find solutions and keep moving forward. A skilled artist knows which tool to use for each part of the painting.

Learning from competitors is like watching how other athletes train for a race. You can observe their strengths and weaknesses to improve your own performance. For example, if a competitor's content goes viral, studying what made it successful can inspire your own ideas. Learning from others helps you stay competitive and find new ways to grow. A smart athlete uses every opportunity to improve their skills.

Using data to guide your decisions is like using a compass to find your direction. The data shows you where you are and helps you decide where to go next. For example, if your engagement is higher in the evening, scheduling your posts for that time can maximize your reach. A good compass keeps you on the right path, even when the journey is challenging. Clear direction makes decision-making easier and more accurate.

Training your team is like sharpening your tools before starting a project. A well-prepared team can handle challenges more effectively and contribute to your growth. For example, teaching your team how to use new social media features ensures that they can create better content. Training keeps everyone up to date and ready to adapt to changes. Sharp tools make the work smoother and more efficient.

Building a strong brand identity is like constructing a house with a solid foundation. When your identity is clear and consistent, it becomes easier for people to recognize and trust you. For example, using the same colors, logo, and tone across all platforms reinforces your brand's image. A strong foundation supports the house through all kinds of weather. A clear identity helps you stand out and grow steadily.

Collaborating with others is like joining forces to build a bridge. Each partner brings their own skills and resources, making the process faster and more effective. For example, partnering with an influencer can introduce your brand to a wider audience and drive more engagement. Collaboration creates opportunities for mutual growth and success. A strong bridge connects you to new possibilities.

Focusing on quality over quantity is like serving a few delicious dishes at a dinner party instead of many average ones. People remember the quality of what you offer more than the number of things you provide. For example, posting fewer but higher-quality posts can create a stronger impact on your audience. Quality builds trust and keeps people coming back for more. A memorable meal leaves a lasting impression.

Taking calculated risks is like crossing a river on stepping stones. Each step requires careful planning, but reaching the other side can lead to new opportunities. For example, trying a bold new campaign might feel risky, but it can also help you stand out and attract attention. Taking smart risks allows you to grow and explore new possibilities. A successful crossing leads to exciting discoveries.

Staying optimistic during challenges is like keeping a lantern lit in the dark. Optimism helps you see the possibilities even when things are uncertain. For example, viewing a temporary drop in sales as a chance to rethink your strategy can lead to better results in the long run. A positive mindset keeps you motivated and focused on solutions. A bright lantern lights the way forward.

Connecting with your audience emotionally is like playing a song that touches people's hearts. When your message resonates on a deeper level, it creates loyalty and trust. For example, sharing a heartfelt story about your brand's journey can inspire your audience and strengthen their connection to you. Emotional connections make your brand unforgettable. A meaningful song stays in people's minds long after it ends.

Planning for the future is like planting seeds that will grow into a forest. Each small action today contributes to long-term success. For example, investing in building an email list now can create a valuable marketing tool in the future. Thinking ahead ensures that you are prepared for whatever changes come your way. A well-planted forest provides shade and resources for years to come.

Keeping your audience engaged is like tending a fire to keep it burning. Regular interaction and fresh content keep the energy alive. For example, responding to comments and sharing new ideas shows your audience that you value their presence. Engagement builds a sense of community and loyalty around your brand. A well-tended fire provides warmth and light for everyone.

Viral Blueprints for Small Business Success

Social Media Marketing

By

Dr. David K. Ewen